MACMILLAN READERS
STARTER LEVEL

W0099664

STEPHEN COLBOURN

The Lost Ship

MACMILLAN

Sunday, December 1872
5th

The weather is fine. The wind is blowing and the ship is sailing quickly. The men are happy. We are sailing between Cuba and Florida. We are going to be in

Florida are going Florid four

We
reach
three or
s.

This is the Captain of the ship. He is in his cabin. He is writing in the ship's log book.

The Captain writes in the log book every day. He writes about the weather and he writes about the ship. He also writes about the men on the ship.

The ship is old. It is a sailing ship. The wind blows and the ship sails.

The Captain and his men are going home. They are going to reach home soon. They are well and happy.

The Captain is shouting, 'Hallo! Is anybody there? Can you hear me? Is anybody there?'

But there is no answer from the strange ship.

Where are the men on the ship? Are they ill?

The Captain gets into a small boat. Two men go in the boat with him. They row across to the strange ship. They are going to look for the men on the ship.

The Captain is on the deck of the strange ship. The two men are with him. They walk along the deck. They go to the ship's wheel.

There is nobody at the wheel. Nobody is steering the ship. The ship is sailing in the wind. The wind is steering the ship.

The Captain shouts,

Is anybody here?

There is no answer. There is nobody on deck.

The Captain is below deck. He is looking for the ship's men. He cannot find them.

Now he is in the cabin where the men eat. There is a table.

There is food on the table. But who is going to eat the food?

There is water in the jug. But who is going to drink the water?

There is a cigar in the ashtray. But who is smoking the cigar?

This is the Captain's cabin. But the Captain is not here. There is nobody in the cabin.

There is a table and a chair. The ship's log book and a photograph are on the table.

The ship's log book is open.

Thursday
25th November 1869
Where are we? Somewhere
in the Atlantic Ocean?
Somewhere between
Bermuda and Florida?
I don't know.
The ship is in a thick,
white mist. I cannot
see the sun or stars.
There is no wind. The
ship is not moving.
Every day I pray for
wind. When will the
wind come?
The men are angry.

They want to
the ship. The
take the sm
They want
Florida. T
go home.

Friday
26th Nov
The men
the sm
going to

Saturd
27th
I am
waiti

12

The Captain reads the log book. He sees the photograph on the table. He picks it up. He looks at the photograph.

No! No! It can't be!

The Captain looks at the photograph. It is a photograph of a man.

The Captain looks in the mirror on the cabin wall. He looks at his face in the mirror. He looks at the face in the photograph. They are the same.

It is a photograph of himself!

The Captain runs up on deck. There is a thick mist around the ship.

The Captain looks around. He can see nobody. He can see nothing.

Where is his ship? Where are his men?

He cannot see the sun. He is alone.

I do not know the date. Where am I? I do not know. I am the Captain of this ship. I must sail the ship. Where am I going? I do not know. What is my name? What is the name of this ship? I do not know. I am waiting... Another Ship is going to com... Another Captai... is going to take my place. The... I can reso... I am waitin...